simple, straightforward recipes

chinese

Contents

The Chinese Kitchen

BAMBOO STRAINER This is a wide, flat, metal strainer with a bamboo handle. It makes removing cooked food from hot oil or water much easier. Of course, an ordinary metal slotted spoon may be used instead.

CHOPSTICKS Food is usually eaten with chopsticks in China. Wooden chopsticks are inexpensive, but plastic ones are more hygienic and can be re-used many times.

CLEAVERS Used to slice, chop, shred, fillet, dice and crush. the cleaver is such an all-purpose tool that skilled Chinese cooks need no other knives, although they may have several weights (light, medium and heavy) of cleaver. The best quality are made with tempered carbon steel so that the blade can be kept razor sharp, although a good-quality stainless steel one is less likely to rust.

ELECTRIC RICE COOKER Since many meals are accompanied by rice, most modern Chinese kitchens have an electric rice cooker. It is the easiest way to cook rice to perfection with little attention.

SPATULA A long-handled spatula with a shovel-shaped end for stir-frying food is relatively inexpensive, although you can use a long-handled wooden spoon if you prefer.

STEAMERS You can either use a stainless steel steamer with small, round perforations that fits over a saucepan, or buy a more traditional bamboo steamer. You will need one or more tiers, plus a lid to fit. It is a good idea to briefly wash the bamboo steamer before using it for the first time and to steam it while empty for a few minutes.

WOK This is probably the most useful and versatile piece of equipment and is used for stir-frying, deep-frying and steaming. The traditional shape has deep, sloping sides and a rounded base to ensure quick, even cooking. In stir-frying, it is possible to move the food around without pieces spilling over the edges, and in deep-frying the rounded shape means that considerably less oil is needed than in a conventional pan. This shape is only suitable for use on a gas hob, however, and if yours is electric, you will need a wok with a flatter base that is specifically designed for such hobs. Woks made of carbon steel can take very high heat without scorching the food. Non-stick woks are also available, allowing you to reduce the fat in many recipes.

COOKING TECHNIQUES AND INGREDIENTS

DEEP-FRYING When deep-frying in a wok, pour in enough oil to come no more than halfway up the wok. Gently heat until the required temperature is reached, preferably using a cooking thermometer. Alternatively, you can test the temperature by dropping in a small cube of bread; bubbles should quickly form all over the surface. Carefully add the

chinese

This is a Star Fire book
First Published in 2005

06 08 09 07 05

1 3 5 7 9 10 8 6 4 2

Star Fire is part of The Foundry Creative Media Company Limited
Crabtree Hall, Crabtree Lane, Fulham, London, SW6 6TY
Please visit the our website: *www.star-fire.co.uk*

Please visit our cookery website: *www.practicalrecipes.com*

ISBN: 1-904041-34-5

The CIP record for this book is available from the British Library

Printed in China

ACKNOWLEDGEMENTS

Authors: Catherine Atkinson, Juliet Barker, Liz Martin,
Gina Steer, Carol Tennant, Mari Mereid Williams,
Elizabeth Wolf-Cohen, Simone Wright

Editorial Consultant: Gina Steer
Project Editor: Sarah Goulding

Editors: Karen Fitzpatrick, Vicky Garrard, Julia Rolf
Photography: Colin Bowling and Paul Forrester

Home Economists and Stylists: Jacqueline Bellefontaine,
Mandy Phipps, Vicki Smallwood and Penny Stephens

Design Team: Lucy Bradbury and Chris Herbert

All props supplied by Barbara Stewart at Surfaces

NOTE

Recipes using uncooked eggs should be avoided by infants, the elderly, pregnant women and anyone suffering from an illness.

food to the oil with tongs or a slotted spoon and move it around occasionally while cooking to keep the pieces separate. It is far better to cook in batches than to add all the food at once, as you may risk the oil bubbling up too much and cause the temperature of the oil to drop, making the outside soggy. Remove the food when cooked and drain on absorbent kitchen paper to soak up any excess oil before serving. Always make sure that the wok is secure before you start cooking and never leave it unattended. A deep-fat fryer is a costly, but useful, piece of equipment if you deep-fry foods often, and you may find it safer and easier to use than a wok.

STEAMING This is a gentle and moist method of cooking, especially good for delicate foods such as fish. It relies on the heat circulating around the food, so make sure you leave a little space between each item, when adding. After arranging, place the steamer above simmering water in a wok or saucepan. To prevent any food sticking to the steamer, you can line it first with a piece of muslin. If desired, add a few slices of fresh ginger to the water and a bay leaf. This not only adds a slight flavouring to the food, but makes a wonderful aroma in the kitchen, and can help mask cooking smells especially if you are steaming fish. Steam for the recommended time and check the water level in the pan or wok occasionally, topping up with more boiling water if necessary. If you do not have a steamer, you can use a wok instead. Place a trivet in the wok and pour in enough boiling water to come to just below the level of the trivet. Place the food to be steamed on a heatproof plate and put on top of the trivet. Cover and steam as before.

STIR-FRYING This quick-cook technique retains the fresh flavour, colour and texture of food. It is essential to have all ingredients prepared before you start cooking. Heat the wok for about a minute over a high heat, then add the oil and swirl it around to coat the base and about halfway up the sides. Continue heating until hot but not smoking, so that when the food is added it starts to cook straight away. Add the ingredients, one at a time, tossing and stirring continuously. Aromatics such as garlic and ginger are usually added first, followed by the main ingredients that need longer cooking such as meat, and finally those that need little cooking or only a brief heating through. Liquids and sauces are usually added towards the end of cooking and then reduced for a minute or two.

SPICE MIXTURES AND FLAVOURINGS Although these can be bought, by making your own basic seasoning mixtures, your finished dishes will have an unmistakable fresh flavour. You will also be able to adjust the spices to suit your individual taste.

CRISPY SEAWEED This is often used as a garnish on Chinese dishes. Finely shred a piece of dark green cabbage – Savoy is ideal – and deep-fry in groundnut oil at 180°C/350°F for about 1 minute until crispy. Sprinkle with a little finely ground sea salt and scatter over the dish or serve separately as a side dish.

Bean & Cashew Stir Fry

Ingredients

Serves 4

3 tbsp sunflower oil
1 onion, peeled and finely chopped
1 celery stalk, trimmed and chopped
2.5 cm/1 inch piece fresh root ginger, peeled and grated
2 garlic cloves, peeled and crushed
1 red chilli, deseeded and finely chopped
175 g/6 oz fine French beans, trimmed and halved
175 g/6 oz mangetout, sliced diagonally into three
75 g/3 oz unsalted cashew nuts
1 tsp brown sugar
125 ml/4 fl oz vegetable stock
2 tbsp dry sherry
1 tbsp light soy sauce
1 tsp red wine vinegar
salt and freshly ground black pepper
freshly chopped coriander, to garnish

1 Heat a wok or large frying pan, add the oil and when hot, add the onion and celery and stir-fry gently for 3–4 minutes or until softened.

2 Add the ginger, garlic and chilli to the wok and stir-fry for 30 seconds. Stir in the French beans and mangetout together with the cashew nuts and continue to stir-fry for 1–2 minutes, or until the nuts are golden brown.

3 Dissolve the sugar in the stock, then blend with the sherry, soy sauce and vinegar. Stir into the bean mixture and bring to the boil. Simmer gently, stirring occasionally for 3–4 minutes, or until the beans and mangetout are tender but still crisp and the sauce has thickened slightly. Season to taste with salt and pepper.

4 Transfer to a warmed serving bowl or spoon on to individual plates. Sprinkle with freshly chopped coriander and serve immediately.

1

2

3

Beef & Baby Corn Stir Fry

Ingredients

Serves 4

3 tbsp light soy sauce
1 tbsp clear honey, warmed
450 g/1 lb beef rump steak, trimmed and thinly sliced
6 tbsp groundnut oil
125 g/4 oz shiitake mushrooms, wiped and halved
125 g/4 oz beansprouts, rinsed
2.5 cm/1 inch piece fresh root ginger, peeled and cut into matchsticks
125 g/4 oz mangetout, halved lengthways
125 g/4 oz broccoli, trimmed and cut into florets
1 medium carrot, peeled and cut into matchsticks
125 g/4 oz baby sweetcorn cobs, halved lengthways
¼ head Chinese leaves, shredded
1 tbsp chilli sauce
3 tbsp black bean sauce
1 tbsp dry sherry
freshly cooked noodles, to serve

1 Mix together the soy sauce and honey in a shallow dish. Add the sliced beef and turn to coat evenly. Cover with clingfilm and leave to marinate for at least 30 minutes, turning occasionally.

2 Heat a wok or large frying pan, add 2 tablespoons of the oil and heat until just smoking. Add the mushrooms and stir-fry for 1 minute. Add the bean sprouts and stir-fry for 1 minute. Using a slotted spoon, transfer the mushroom mixture to a plate and keep warm.

3 Drain the beef, reserving the marinade. Reheat the wok, pour in 2 tablespoons of the oil and heat until smoking. Add the beef and stir-fry for 4 minutes or until browned. Transfer to a plate and keep warm.

4 Add the remaining oil to the wok and heat until just smoking. Add the ginger, mangetout, broccoli, carrot and the baby sweetcorn with the shredded Chinese leaves and stir-fry for 3 minutes. Stir in the chilli and black bean sauces, the sherry, the reserved marinade and the beef and mushroom mixture. Stir-fry for 2 minutes, then serve immediately with freshly cooked noodles.

1

2

4

Braised Chicken with Aubergine

Ingredients

Serves 4

- 3 tbsp vegetable oil
- 12 chicken thighs
- 2 large aubergines, trimmed and cubed
- 4 garlic cloves, peeled and crushed
- 2 tsp freshly grated root ginger
- 900 ml/1½ pints vegetable stock
- 2 tbsp light soy sauce
- 2 tbsp Chinese preserved black beans
- 6 spring onions, trimmed and thinly sliced diagonally
- 1 tbsp cornflour
- 1 tbsp sesame oil
- spring onion tassels, to garnish
- freshly cooked noodles or rice, to serve

1 Heat a wok or large frying pan, add the oil and when hot, add the chicken thighs and cook over a medium high heat for 5 minutes, or until browned all over. Transfer to a large plate and keep warm.

2 Add the aubergine to the wok and cook over a high heat for 5 minutes or until browned, turning occasionally. Add the garlic and ginger and stir-fry for 1 minute.

3 Return the chicken to the wok, pour in the stock and add the soy sauce and black beans. Bring to the boil, then simmer for 20 minutes, or until the chicken is tender. Add the spring onions after 10 minutes.

4 Blend the cornflour with 2 tablespoons of water. Stir into the wok and simmer until the sauce has thickened. Stir in the sesame oil, heat for 30 seconds, then remove from the heat. Garnish with spring onion tassels and serve immediately with noodles or rice.

CHEF'S TIP

Make your own Chinese-style vegetable stock using basic stock ingredients and then adding a few dried shiitake mushrooms and some slices of fresh root ginger.

Chinese Barbecue-style Quails with Aubergines

Ingredients

Serves 6

4 quails
2 tbsp salt
3 tbsp hoisin sauce
1 tbsp Chinese rice wine or dry sherry
1 tbsp light soy sauce
700 g/1½ lb aubergines, trimmed and cubed
1 tbsp oil
4 garlic cloves, peeled and finely chopped
1 tbsp freshly chopped root ginger
6 spring onions, trimmed and finely chopped
3 tbsp dark soy sauce
¼ tsp dried chilli flakes
1 tbsp yellow bean sauce
1 tbsp sugar

To garnish:

sprigs of fresh coriander
sliced red chilli

2

1 Preheat the oven to 240°C/475°F/Gas Mark 9. Rub the quails inside and out with 1 tablespoon of the salt. Mix together the hoisin sauce, Chinese rice wine or sherry and light soy sauce. Rub the quails inside and out with the sauce. Transfer to a small roasting tin and roast in the preheated oven for 5 minutes. Reduce the heat to 180°C/350°F/Gas Mark 4 and continue to roast for 20 minutes. Turn the oven off and leave the quails for 5 minutes, then remove and leave to rest for 10 minutes.

2 Place the aubergine in a colander and sprinkle with the remaining salt. Leave to drain for 20 minutes, then rinse under cold running water and pat dry with absorbent kitchen paper.

3 Heat a wok or large frying pan over a moderate heat. Add the oil and when hot, add the aubergines, garlic, ginger and four of the spring onions and cook for 1 minute. Add the dark soy sauce, chilli flakes, yellow bean sauce, sugar and 450 ml/¾ pint of water. Bring to the boil, then simmer uncovered for 10–15 minutes.

4 Increase the heat to high and continue to cook, stirring occasionally, until the sauce is reduced and slightly thickened. Spoon the aubergine mixture on to warmed individual plates and top with a quail. Garnish with the remaining spring onion, fresh chilli and a sprig of coriander and serve immediately.

Chinese Leaves with Sweet & Sour Sauce

Ingredients
Serves 4

1 head Chinese leaves
200 g pack pak choi
1 tbsp cornflour
1 tbsp soy sauce
2 tbsp brown sugar
3 tbsp red wine vinegar
3 tbsp orange juice
2 tbsp tomato purée
3 tbsp sunflower oil
15 g/½ oz butter
1 tsp salt
2 tbsp toasted sesame seeds

1 Discard any tough outer leaves and stalks from the Chinese leaves and pak choi and wash well. Drain thoroughly and pat dry with absorbent kitchen paper. Shred the Chinese leaves and pak choi lengthways. Reserve.

2 In a small bowl, blend the cornflour with 4 tablespoons of water. Add the soy sauce, sugar, vinegar, orange juice and tomato purée and stir until blended thoroughly.

3 Pour the sauce into a small saucepan and bring to the boil. Simmer gently for 2–3 minutes, or until the sauce is thickened and smooth.

4 Meanwhile, heat a wok or large frying pan and add the sunflower oil and butter. When melted, add the prepared Chinese leaves and pak choi, sprinkle with the salt and stir-fry for 2 minutes. Reduce the heat and cook gently for a further 1–2 minutes or until tender.

5 Transfer the Chinese leaves and pak choi to a warmed serving platter and drizzle over the warm sauce. Sprinkle with the toasted sesame seeds and serve immediately.

Chinese Salad with Soy & Ginger Dressing

Ingredients
Serves 4

1 head of Chinese cabbage
200 g can water chestnuts, drained
6 spring onions, trimmed
4 ripe but firm cherry tomatoes
125 g/4 oz mangetout
125 g/4 oz beansprouts
2 tbsp freshly chopped coriander

For the soy and ginger dressing:

2 tbsp sunflower oil
4 tbsp light soy sauce
2.5 cm/1 inch piece root ginger, peeled and finely grated
zest and juice of 1 lemon
salt and freshly ground black pepper
crusty white bread, to serve

CHEF'S TIP
Sprinkling the tomatoes with a small amount of sugar will draw out the bitter juices, and add an intensity to the flavour. Be sure to drain off the juices before serving.

1 Rinse and finely shred the Chinese cabbage and place in a serving dish.

2 Slice the water chestnuts into small slivers and cut the spring onions diagonally into 2.5 cm/1 inch lengths, then split lengthwise into thin strips.

3 Cut the tomatoes in half and then slice each half into three wedges and reserve.

4 Simmer the mangetout in boiling water for 2 minutes until beginning to soften, drain and cut in half diagonally.

5 Arrange the water chestnuts, spring onions, mangetout, tomatoes and beansprouts on top of the shredded Chinese cabbage. Garnish with the freshly chopped coriander.

6 Make the dressing by whisking all the ingredients together in a small bowl until mixed thoroughly. Serve with the bread and the salad.

2

3

5

Chinese Steamed Sea Bass with Black Beans

Ingredients

Serves 4

- 1.1 kg/2½ lb sea bass, cleaned with head and tail left on
- 1–2 tbsp rice wine or dry sherry
- 1½ tbsp groundnut oil
- 2–3 tbsp fermented black beans, rinsed and drained
- 1 garlic clove, peeled and finely chopped
- 1 cm/½ inch piece fresh root ginger, peeled and finely chopped
- 4 spring onions, trimmed and thinly sliced diagonally
- 2–3 tbsp soy sauce
- 125 ml/4 fl oz fish or chicken stock
- 1–2 tbsp sweet Chinese chilli sauce, or to taste
- 2 tsp sesame oil
- sprigs of fresh coriander, to garnish

1

1 Using a sharp knife, cut 3–4 deep diagonal slashes along both sides of the fish. Sprinkle the Chinese rice wine or sherry inside and over the fish and gently rub into the skin on both sides.

2 Lightly brush a heatproof plate large enough to fit into a large wok or frying pan with a little of the groundnut oil. Place the fish on the plate, curving the fish along the inside edge of the dish, then leave for 20 minutes.

3 Place a wire rack or inverted ramekin in the wok and pour in enough water to come about 2.5 cm/1 inch up the side. Bring to the boil over a high heat.

4 Carefully place the plate with the fish on the rack or ramekin, cover and steam for 12–15 minutes, or until the fish is tender and the flesh is opaque when pierced with a knife near the bone.

5 Remove the plate with the fish from the wok and keep warm. Remove the rack or ramekin from the wok and pour off the water. Return the wok to the heat, add the remaining groundnut oil and swirl to coat the bottom and side. Add the black beans, garlic and ginger and stir-fry for 1 minute.

6 Add the spring onions, soy sauce, fish or chicken stock and boil for 1 minute. Stir in the chilli sauce and sesame oil, then pour the sauce over the cooked fish. Garnish with coriander sprigs and serve immediately.

Clear Chicken & Mushroom Soup

Ingredients

Serves 4

2 large chicken legs, about 450 g/1 lb total weight
1 tbsp groundnut oil
1 tsp sesame oil
1 onion, peeled and very thinly sliced
2.5 cm/1 inch piece root ginger, peeled and very finely chopped
1.1 litres/2 pints clear chicken stock
1 lemon grass stalk, bruised
50 g/2 oz long-grain rice
75 g/3 oz button mushrooms, wiped and finely sliced
4 spring onions, trimmed, cut into 5 cm/2 inch pieces and shredded
1 tbsp dark soy sauce
4 tbsp dry sherry
salt and freshly ground black pepper

CHEF'S TIP

Miso is a tasty and nutritious alternative to chicken stock.

1 Skin the chicken legs and remove any fat. Cut each in half to make two thigh and two drumstick portions and reserve. Heat the groundnut and sesame oils in a large saucepan. Add the sliced onion and cook gently for 10 minutes, or until soft but not beginning to colour.

2 Add the chopped ginger to the saucepan and cook for about 30 seconds, stirring all the time to prevent it sticking, then pour in the stock. Add the chicken pieces and the lemon grass, cover and simmer gently for 15 minutes. Stir in the rice and cook for a further 15 minutes or until the chicken is cooked.

3 Remove the chicken from the saucepan and leave until cool enough to handle. Finely shred the flesh, then return to the saucepan with the mushrooms, spring onions, soy sauce and sherry. Simmer for 5 minutes, or until the rice and mushrooms are tender. Remove the lemon grass.

4 Season the soup to taste with salt and pepper. Ladle into warmed serving bowls, making sure each has an equal amount of shredded chicken and vegetables and serve immediately.

1

2

3

Corn Fritters with Hot & Spicy Relish

Ingredients
Makes 16–20

For the spicy relish:

3 tbsp sunflower oil
1 onion, peeled and very finely chopped
¼ tsp dried crushed chillies
2 garlic cloves, peeled and crushed
2 tbsp plum sauce

For the fritters:

325 g can sweetcorn kernels, drained
1 onion, peeled and very finely chopped
1 spring onion, trimmed and very finely chopped
½ tsp chilli powder
1 tsp ground coriander
4 tbsp plain flour
1 tsp baking powder
1 medium egg
salt and freshly ground black pepper
300 ml/½ pint groundnut oil
sprigs of fresh coriander, to garnish

1 To make the relish, heat a wok, add the sunflower oil and when hot, add the onion and stir-fry for 3–4 minutes or until softened. Add the chillies and garlic, stir-fry for 1 minute, then leave to cool slightly. Stir in the plum sauce, transfer to a food processor and blend until the consistency of chutney. Reserve.

2 For the fritters, place the sweetcorn into a food processor and blend briefly until just mashed. Transfer to a bowl with the onions, chilli powder, coriander, flour, baking powder and egg. Season to taste with salt and pepper and mix together.

3 Heat a wok, add the oil and heat to 180°C/350°F. Working in batches, drop a few spoonfuls of the sweetcorn mixture into the oil and deep-fry for 3–4 minutes, or until golden and crispy, turning occasionally. Using a slotted spoon, remove and drain on absorbent kitchen paper. Arrange on a warmed serving platter, garnish with sprigs of coriander and serve immediately with the relish.

1

2

3

Crispy Pork Wontons

Ingredients
Serves 4

1 small onion, peeled and roughly chopped
2 garlic cloves, peeled and crushed
1 green chilli, deseeded and chopped
2.5 cm/1 inch piece fresh root ginger, peeled and roughly chopped
450 g/1 lb lean pork mince
4 tbsp freshly chopped coriander
1 tsp Chinese five spice powder
salt and freshly ground black pepper
20 wonton wrappers
1 medium egg, lightly beaten
vegetable oil for deep-frying
chilli sauce, to serve

CHEF'S TIP
To check whether the oil is hot enough for deep-frying, drop a cube of day-old bread into the oil. It will turn golden-brown in 45 seconds if the temperature is correct.

1 Place the onion, garlic, chilli and ginger in a food processor and blend until very finely chopped. Add the pork, coriander and Chinese five spice powder. Season to taste with salt and pepper, then blend again briefly to mix. Divide the mixture into 20 equal portions and with floured hands shape each into a walnut-sized ball.

2 Brush the edges of a wonton wrapper with beaten egg, place a pork ball in the centre, then bring the corners to the centre and pinch together to make a money bag. Repeat with the remaining pork balls and wrappers.

3 Pour sufficient oil into a heavy-based saucepan or deep-fat fryer so that it is one-third full and heat to 180°C/350°F. Deep-fry the wontons in three or four batches for 3–4 minutes, or until cooked through and golden and crisp. Drain on absorbent kitchen paper. Serve the crispy pork wontons immediately, allowing five per person, with some chilli sauce for dipping.

1

2

3

Crispy Prawns with Chinese Dipping Sauce

Ingredients
Serves 4

450 g/1 lb medium-sized raw prawns, peeled
¼ tsp salt
6 tbsp groundnut oil
2 garlic cloves, peeled and finely chopped
2.5 cm/1 inch piece fresh root ginger, peeled and finely chopped
1 green chilli, deseeded and finely chopped
4 stems fresh coriander, leaves and stems roughly chopped

For the chinese dipping sauce:

3 tbsp dark soy sauce
3 tbsp rice wine vinegar
1 tbsp caster sugar
2 tbsp chilli oil
2 spring onions, finely shredded

CHEF'S TIP
Although you must cook raw prawns thoroughly, it is equally important not to overcook them or they will become tough and chewy and lose their delicate flavour.

1 Using a sharp knife, remove the black vein along the back of the prawns. Sprinkle the prawns with the salt and leave to stand for 15 minutes. Pat dry on absorbent kitchen paper.

2 Heat a wok or large frying pan, add the groundnut oil and when hot, add the prawns and stir-fry in two batches for about 1 minute, or until they turn pink and are almost cooked. Using a slotted spoon, remove the prawns and keep warm in a low oven.

3 Drain the oil from the wok, leaving 1 tablespoon. Add the garlic, ginger and chilli and cook for about 30 seconds. Add the coriander, return the prawns and stir-fry for 1–2 minutes, or until the prawns are cooked through and the garlic is golden. Turn into a warmed serving dish.

4 For the dipping sauce, using a fork, beat together the soy sauce, rice vinegar, caster sugar and chilli oil in a small bowl. Stir in the spring onions. Serve immediately with the hot prawns.

2

3

4

Crispy Roast Duck Legs with Pancakes

Ingredients

Serves 6

900 g/2 lb plums, halved
25 g/1 oz butter
2 star anise
1 tsp freshly grated root ginger
50 g/2 oz soft brown sugar
zest and juice of 1 orange
salt and freshly ground black pepper
4 duck legs
3 tbsp dark soy sauce
2 tbsp dark brown sugar
½ cucumber, cut into matchsticks
1 small bunch spring onions, trimmed and shredded
18 ready-made Chinese pancakes, warmed

3

1 Preheat the oven to 220°C/425°F/Gas Mark 7, 15 minutes before cooking. Discard stones from plums and place in a saucepan with the butter, star anise, ginger, brown sugar and orange zest and juice. Season to taste with pepper. Cook over a gentle heat until the sugar has dissolved. Bring to the boil, then reduce heat and simmer for 15 minutes, stirring occasionally until the plums are soft and the mixture is thick. Remove the star anise and leave to cool.

2 Using a fork, prick the duck legs all over. Place in a large bowl and pour boiling water over to remove some of the fat. Drain, pat dry on absorbent kitchen paper and leave until cold.

3 Mix together the soy sauce, dark brown sugar and the ½ teaspoon of salt. Rub this mixture generously over the duck legs. Transfer to a wire rack set over a roasting tin and roast in the preheated oven for 30–40 minutes, or until well cooked and the skin is browned and crisp. Remove from the oven and leave to rest for 10 minutes.

4 Shred the duck meat using a fork to hold the hot duck leg and another to remove the meat. Transfer to a warmed serving platter with the cucumber and spring onions. Serve immediately with the plum compote and warmed pancakes.

Duck in Black Bean Sauce

Ingredients
Serves 4

- 450 g/1 lb duck breast, skinned
- 1 tbsp light soy sauce
- 1 tbsp Chinese rice wine or dry sherry
- 2.5 cm/1 inch piece fresh root ginger
- 3 garlic cloves
- 2 spring onions
- 2 tbsp Chinese preserved black beans
- 1 tbsp groundnut or vegetable oil
- 150 ml/¼ pint chicken stock
- shredded spring onions, to garnish
- freshly cooked noodles, to serve

1 Using a sharp knife, trim the duck breasts, removing any fat. Slice thickly and place in a shallow dish. Mix together the soy sauce and Chinese rice wine or sherry and pour over the duck. Leave to marinate for 1 hour in the refrigerator, then drain and discard the marinade.

2 Peel the ginger and chop finely. Peel the garlic cloves and either chop finely or crush. Trim the root from the spring onions, discard the outer leaves and chop. Finely chop the black beans.

3 Heat a wok or large frying pan, add the oil and when very hot, add the ginger, garlic, spring onions and black beans and stir-fry for 30 seconds. Add the drained duck and stir-fry for 3–5 minutes or until the duck is browned.

4 Add the chicken stock to the wok, bring to the boil, then reduce the heat and simmer for 5 minutes, or until the duck is cooked and the sauce is reduced and thickened. Remove from the heat. Tip on to a bed of freshly cooked noodles, garnish with spring onion shreds and serve immediately.

CHEF'S TIP

For spring onion shreds, cut off most of the white bulb end, trim the tops and cut the remaining green parts lengthways into fine strips. To make them curl, drop into iced water for a few minutes.

1

3

4

Hoisin Duck & Greens Stir-Fry

Ingredients

Serves 4

350 g/12 oz duck breasts, skinned and cut into strips
1 medium egg white, beaten
½ tsp salt
1 tsp sesame oil
2 tsp cornflour
2 tbsp groundnut oil
2 tbsp freshly grated root ginger
50 g/2 oz bamboo shoots
50 g/2 oz fine green beans, trimmed
50 g/2 oz pak choi, trimmed
2 tbsp hoisin sauce
1 tsp Chinese rice wine or dry sherry
zest and juice of ½ orange
strips of orange zest, to garnish
freshly steamed egg noodles, to serve

1 Place the duck strips in a shallow dish, then add the egg white, salt, sesame oil and cornflour. Stir lightly until the duck is coated in the mixture. Cover and chill in the refrigerator for 20 minutes.

2 Heat the wok until very hot and add the oil. Remove the wok from the heat and add the duck, stirring continuously to prevent the duck from sticking to the wok. Add the ginger and stir-fry for 2 minutes. Add the bamboo shoots, the green beans and the pak choi, and stir-fry for 1–2 minutes until wilted.

3 Mix together the hoisin sauce, the Chinese rice wine or sherry and the orange zest and juice. Pour into the wok and stir to coat the duck and vegetables. Stir-fry for 1–2 minutes, or until the duck and vegetables are tender. Garnish with the strips of orange zest and serve immediately with freshly steamed egg noodles.

CHEF'S TIP

Duck breasts are usually sold with the skin on, but it can easily be removed by inserting a sharp knife between the skin and the meat.

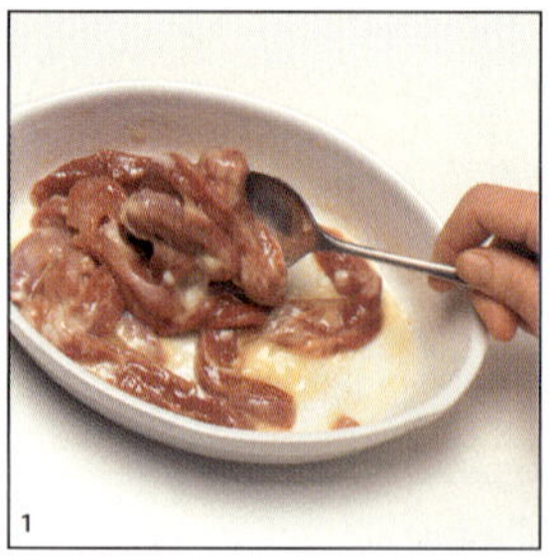

1

2

3

Hot & Sour Mushroom Soup

Ingredients

Serves 4

4 tbsp sunflower oil
3 garlic cloves, peeled and finely chopped
3 shallots, peeled and finely chopped
2 large red chillies, deseeded and finely chopped
1 tbsp soft brown sugar
large pinch of salt
1 litre/1¾ pints vegetable stock
250 g/9 oz Thai fragrant rice
5 kaffir lime leaves, torn
2 tbsp soy sauce
grated rind and juice of 1 lemon
250 g/9 oz oyster mushrooms, wiped and cut into pieces
2 tbsp freshly chopped coriander

To garnish:

2 green chillies, deseeded and finely chopped
3 spring onions, trimmed and finely chopped

1 Heat the oil in a frying pan, add the garlic and shallots and cook until golden brown and starting to crisp. Remove from the pan and reserve. Add the chillies to the pan and cook until they start to change colour.

2 Place the garlic, shallots and chillies in a food processor or blender and blend to a smooth purée with 150 ml/¼ pint water. Pour the purée back into the pan, add the sugar with a large pinch of salt, then cook gently, stirring, until dark in colour. Take care not to burn the mixture.

3 Pour the stock into a large saucepan, add the garlic purée, rice, lime leaves, soy sauce and the lemon rind and juice. Bring to the boil, then reduce the heat, cover and simmer gently for about 10 minutes.

4 Add the mushrooms and simmer for a further 10 minutes, or until the mushrooms and rice are tender. Remove the lime leaves, stir in the chopped coriander and ladle into bowls. Place the chopped green chillies and spring onions in small bowls and serve separately to sprinkle on top of the soup.

1

2

4

Lamb with Stir-fried Vegetables

Ingredients

Serves 4

- 550 g/1¼ lb lamb fillet, cut into strips
- 2.5 cm/1 inch piece fresh root ginger, peeled and cut into matchsticks
- 2 garlic cloves, peeled and chopped
- 4 tbsp soy sauce
- 2 tbsp dry sherry
- 2 tsp cornflour
- 4 tbsp groundnut oil
- 75 g/3 oz French beans, trimmed and cut in half
- 2 medium carrots, peeled and cut into matchsticks
- 1 red pepper, deseeded and cut into chunks
- 1 yellow pepper, deseeded and cut into chunks
- 225 g can water chestnuts, drained and halved
- 3 tomatoes, chopped
- freshly cooked sticky rice in banana leaves, to serve (optional)

1 Place the lamb strips in a shallow dish. Mix together the ginger and half the garlic in a small bowl. Pour over the soy sauce and sherry and stir well. Pour over the lamb and stir until coated lightly. Cover with clingfilm and leave to marinate for at least 30 minutes, occasionally spooning the marinade over the lamb.

2 Using a slotted spoon, lift the lamb from the marinade and place on a plate. Blend the cornflour and the marinade together until smooth and reserve.

3 Heat a wok or large frying pan, add 2 tablespoons of the oil and when hot, add the remaining garlic, French beans, carrots and peppers and stir-fry for 5 minutes. Using a slotted spoon, transfer the vegetables to a plate and keep warm.

4 Heat the remaining oil in the wok, add the lamb and stir-fry for 2 minutes or until tender. Return the vegetables to the wok with the water chestnuts, tomatoes and reserved marinade mixture. Bring to the boil then simmer for 1 minute. Serve immediately with freshly cooked sticky rice in banana leaves, if liked.

1

3

4

Lime & Sesame Turkey

Ingredients
Serves 4

- 450 g/1 lb turkey breast, skinned and cut into strips
- 2 lemon grass stalks, outer leaves discarded and finely sliced
- grated zest of 1 lime
- 4 garlic cloves, peeled and crushed
- 6 shallots, peeled and finely sliced
- 2 tbsp Thai fish sauce
- 2 tsp soft brown sugar
- 1 small red chilli, deseeded and finely sliced
- 3 tbsp sunflower oil
- 1 tbsp sesame oil
- 225 g/8 oz stir-fry rice noodles
- 1 tbsp sesame seeds
- shredded spring onions, to garnish
- freshly stir-fried vegetables, to serve

CHEF'S TIP

You could vary this recipe by substituting chicken or prawns for the turkey.

1 Place the turkey strips in a shallow dish. Mix together the lemon grass stalks, lime zest, garlic, shallots, Thai fish sauce, sugar and chilli with 2 tablespoons of the sunflower oil and the sesame oil. Pour over the turkey. Cover and leave to marinate in the refrigerator for 2–3 hours, spooning the marinade over the turkey occasionally.

2 Soak the noodles in warm water for 5 minutes. Drain through a sieve or colander, then plunge immediately into cold water. Drain again and reserve until ready to use.

3 Heat the wok until very hot and add the sesame seeds. Dry fry for 1–2 minutes, or until toasted in colour. Remove from the wok and reserve. Wipe the wok to remove any dust left from the seeds.

4 Heat the wok again and add the remaining sunflower oil. When hot, drain the turkey from the marinade and stir-fry for 3–4 minutes, or until golden brown and cooked through. You may need to do this in two batches. When all the turkey has been cooked, add the noodles to the wok and cook, stirring, for 1–2 minutes, or until heated through thoroughly. Garnish with the shredded spring onions and toasted sesame seeds and serve immediately with freshly stir-fried vegetables of your choice.

1

3

4

Mixed Vegetables Stir Fry

Ingredients

Serves 4

2 tbsp groundnut oil
4 garlic cloves, peeled and finely sliced
2.5 cm/1 inch piece of fresh root ginger, peeled and finely sliced
75 g/3 oz broccoli florets
50 g/2 oz mangetout, trimmed
75 g/3 oz carrots, peeled and cut into matchsticks
1 green pepper, deseeded and cut into strips
1 red pepper, deseeded and cut into strips
1 tbsp soy sauce
1 tbsp hoisin sauce
1 tsp sugar
salt and freshly ground black pepper
4 spring onions, trimmed and shredded, to garnish

CHEF'S TIP

If you prefer a more subtle ginger flavour, slice it thickly instead of grating it. Add it to the dish when cooking and remove just before serving.

1 Heat a wok, add the oil and when hot, add the garlic and ginger slices and stir-fry for 1 minute.

2 Add the broccoli florets to the wok, stir-fry for 1 minute, then add the mangetout, carrots and the green and red peppers and stir-fry for a further 3–4 minutes, or until tender but still crisp.

3 Blend the soy sauce, hoisin sauce and sugar in a small bowl. Stir well, season to taste with salt and pepper and pour into the wok. Transfer the vegetables to a warmed serving dish. Garnish with shredded spring onions and serve immediately.

1

2

3

Moo Shi Pork

Ingredients
Serves 4

175 g/6 oz pork fillet
2 tsp Chinese rice wine or dry sherry
2 tbsp light soy sauce
1 tsp cornflour
25 g/1 oz dried golden needles, soaked and drained
2 tbsp groundnut oil
3 medium eggs, lightly beaten
1 tsp freshly grated root ginger
3 spring onions, trimmed and thinly sliced
150 g/5 oz bamboo shoots, cut into fine strips
salt and freshly ground black pepper
8 mandarin pancakes, steamed
hoisin sauce
sprigs of fresh coriander, to garnish

1 Cut the pork across the grain into 1 cm/½ inch slices, then cut into thin strips. Place in a bowl with the Chinese rice wine or sherry, soy sauce and cornflour. Mix well and reserve. Trim off the tough ends of the golden needles, then cut in half and reserve.

2 Heat a wok or large frying pan, add 1 tablespoon of the groundnut oil and when hot, add the lightly beaten eggs, and cook for 1 minute, stirring all the time, until scrambled. Remove and reserve. Wipe the wok clean with absorbent kitchen paper.

3 Return the wok to the heat, add the remaining oil and when hot transfer the pork strips from the marinade mixture to the wok, shaking off as much marinade as possible. Stir-fry for 30 seconds, then add the ginger, spring onions and bamboo shoots and pour in the marinade. Stir-fry for 2–3 minutes or until cooked.

4 Return the scrambled eggs to the wok, season to taste with salt and pepper and stir for a few seconds until mixed well and heated through. Divide the mixture between the pancakes, drizzle each with 1 teaspoon of hoisin sauce and roll up. Garnish and serve immediately.

CHEF'S TIP
If you prefer not to use golden needles, or cannot find them in the shops, omit them and increase the quantity of pork to 225 g/8 oz.

1

2

3

Pork Fried Noodles

Ingredients
Serves 4

- 125 g/4 oz dried thread egg noodles
- 125 g/4 oz broccoli florets
- 4 tbsp groundnut oil
- 350 g/12 oz pork tenderloin, cut into slices
- 3 tbsp soy sauce
- 1 tbsp lemon juice
- pinch of sugar
- 1 tsp chilli sauce
- 1 tbsp sesame oil
- 2.5 cm/1 inch piece fresh root ginger, peeled and cut into sticks
- 1 garlic clove, peeled and chopped
- 1 green chilli, deseeded and sliced
- 125 g/4 oz mangetout, halved
- 2 medium eggs, lightly beaten
- 227 g can water chestnuts, drained and sliced

To garnish:
- radish rose
- spring onion tassels

CHEF'S TIP
Make radish roses by topping and tailing the radishes, making small slits from the top to the base and then plunging them into iced water for 30 minutes.

1 Place the noodles in a bowl and cover with boiling water. Leave to stand for 20 minutes, stirring occasionally, until tender. Drain and reserve. Meanwhile, blanch the broccoli in a saucepan of lightly salted boiling water for 2 minutes. Drain, refresh under cold running water and reserve.

2 Heat a large wok or frying pan, add the groundnut oil and heat until just smoking. Add the pork and stir-fry for 5 minutes, or until browned. Using a slotted spoon, remove the pork slices and reserve.

3 Mix together the soy sauce, lemon juice, sugar, chilli sauce and sesame oil and reserve.

4 Add the ginger to the wok and stir-fry for 30 seconds. Add the garlic and chilli and stir-fry for 30 seconds. Add the reserved broccoli and stir-fry for 3 minutes. Stir in the mangetout, pork and reserved noodles with the beaten eggs and water chestnuts and stir-fry for 5 minutes or until heated through. Pour over the reserved chilli sauce, toss well and turn into a warmed serving dish. Garnish and serve immediately.

Pork Spring Rolls

Ingredients

Serves 4

125 g/4 oz pork tenderloin
2 tbsp light soy sauce
225 ml/8 fl oz groundnut oil
1 medium carrot, peeled and cut into matchsticks
75 g/3 oz button mushrooms, wiped and sliced
4 spring onions, trimmed and thinly sliced
75 g/3 oz beansprouts
1 garlic clove, peeled and chopped
1 tbsp dark soy sauce
12 large sheets filo pastry, folded in half
spring onion curls, to garnish
Chinese-style dipping sauce, to serve

2

1 Trim the pork, discarding any sinew or fat, and cut into very fine strips. Place in a small bowl, pour over the light soy sauce and stir until well coated. Cover with clingfilm and leave to marinate in the refrigerator for at least 30 minutes.

2 Heat a wok or large frying pan, add 1 tablespoon of the oil and when hot, add the carrot and mushrooms and stir-fry for 3 minutes or until softened. Add the spring onions, beansprouts and garlic, stir-fry for 2 minutes, then transfer the vegetables to a bowl and reserve.

3 Drain the pork well, add to the wok and stir-fry for 2–4 minutes or until browned. Add the pork to the vegetables and leave to cool. Stir in the dark soy sauce and mix the filling well.

4 Lay the folded filo pastry sheets on a work surface. Divide the filling between the sheets, placing it at one end. Brush the filo edges with water, then fold the sides over and roll up.

5 Heat the remaining oil in a large wok to 180°C/350°F and cook the spring rolls in batches for 2–3 minutes, or until golden, turning the rolls during cooking. Using a slotted spoon, remove and drain on absorbent kitchen paper. Garnish with spring onion curls and serve immediately with a Chinese-style dipping sauce.

Shredded Beef in Hoisin Sauce

Ingredients

Serves 4

2 celery sticks
125 g/4 oz carrots
450 g/1 lb rump steak
2 tbsp cornflour
salt and freshly ground black pepper
2 tbsp sunflower oil
4 spring onions, trimmed and chopped
2 tbsp light soy sauce
1 tbsp hoisin sauce
1 tbsp sweet chilli sauce
2 tbsp dry sherry
250 g pack fine egg thread noodles
1 tbsp freshly chopped coriander

1 Trim the celery and peel the carrots, then cut into fine matchsticks and reserve.

2 Place the steak between two sheets of greaseproof paper or baking parchment. Beat the steak with a meat mallet or rolling pin until very thin, then slice into strips. Season the cornflour with salt and pepper and use to coat the steak. Reserve.

3 Heat a wok, add the oil and when hot, add the spring onions and cook for 1 minute, then add the steak and stir-fry for a further 3–4 minutes, or until the meat is sealed.

4 Add the celery and carrot matchsticks to the wok and stir-fry for a further 2 minutes before adding the soy, hoisin and chilli sauces and the sherry. Bring to the boil and simmer for 2–3 minutes, or until the steak is tender and the vegetables are cooked.

5 Plunge the fine egg noodles into boiling water and leave for 4 minutes. Drain, then spoon onto a large serving dish. Top with the cooked shredded steak, then sprinkle with chopped coriander and serve immediately.

CHEF'S TIP
Although this recipe calls for dry sherry, chinese rice wine is preferable, if you can find it.

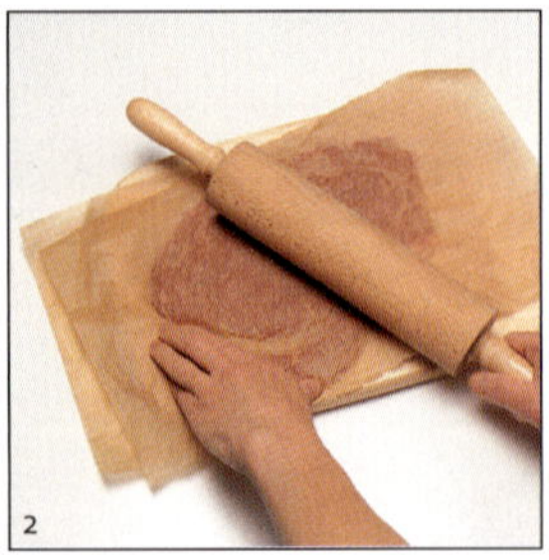
2

3

4

Special Fried Rice

Ingredients
Serves 4

- 25 g/1 oz butter
- 4 medium eggs, beaten
- 4 tbsp vegetable oil
- 1 bunch spring onions, trimmed and shredded
- 225 g/8 oz cooked ham, diced
- 125 g/4 oz large cooked prawns with tails left on
- 75 g/3 oz peas, thawed if frozen
- 200 g can water chestnuts, drained and roughly chopped
- 450 g/1 lb cooked long-grain rice
- 3 tbsp dark soy sauce
- 1 tbsp dry sherry
- 2 tbsp freshly chopped coriander
- salt and freshly ground black pepper

1 Melt the butter in a wok or large frying pan and pour in half the beaten egg. Cook for 4 minutes drawing the edges of the omelette in to allow the uncooked egg to set into a round shape. Using a fish slice, lift the omelette from the wok and roll into a sausage shape. Leave to cool completely then using a sharp knife slice the omelette into rings.

2 Wipe the wok with absorbent kitchen paper and return to the heat. Add the oil and when hot, add the spring onions, ham, prawns, peas and chopped water chestnuts and stir-fry for 2 minutes. Add the rice and stir-fry for a further 3 minutes.

3 Add the remaining beaten eggs and stir-fry for 3 minutes, or until the egg has scrambled and set. Stir in the soy sauce, sherry and chopped coriander. Season to taste with salt and pepper and heat through thoroughly. Add the omelette rings and gently stir without breaking up the egg too much. Serve immediately.

CHEF'S TIP

In Chinese cuisine, rice is always cooked by the absorption method, rather than in large quantities of boiling water, so that all the flavour and nutrients are retained.

Speedy Pork with Yellow Bean Sauce

Ingredients

Serves 4

450 g/1 lb pork fillet
2 tbsp light soy sauce
2 tbsp orange juice
2 tsp cornflour
3 tbsp groundnut oil
2 garlic cloves, peeled and crushed
175 g/6 oz carrots, peeled and cut into matchsticks
125 g/4 oz fine green beans, trimmed and halved
2 spring onions, trimmed and cut into strips
4 tbsp yellow bean sauce
1 tbsp freshly chopped flat leaf parsley, to garnish
freshly cooked egg noodles, to serve

CHEF'S TIP

Black bean sauce could be used as an alternative to the yellow bean sauce in this recipe.

1 Remove any fat or sinew from the pork fillet, and cut into thin strips. Blend the soy sauce, orange juice and cornflour in a bowl and mix thoroughly. Place the meat in a shallow dish, pour over the soy sauce mixture, cover and leave to marinate in the refrigerator for 1 hour. Drain with a slotted spoon, reserving the marinade.

2 Heat the wok, then add 2 tablespoons of the oil and stir-fry the pork with the garlic for 2 minutes, or until the meat is sealed. Remove with a slotted spoon and reserve.

3 Add the remaining oil to the wok and cook the carrots, beans and spring onions for about 3 minutes, until tender but still crisp. Return the pork to the wok with the reserved marinade, then pour over the yellow bean sauce. Stir-fry for a further 1–2 minutes, or until the pork is tender. Sprinkle with the chopped parsley and serve immediately with freshly cooked egg noodles.

Stir-fried Lemon Chicken

Ingredients
Serves 4

- 350 g/12 oz boneless, skinless chicken breast
- 1 large egg white
- 5 tsp cornflour
- 3 tbsp vegetable or groundnut oil
- 150 ml/¼ pint chicken stock
- 2 tbsp fresh lemon juice
- 2 tbsp light soy sauce
- 1 tbsp Chinese rice wine or dry sherry
- 1 tbsp sugar
- 2 garlic cloves, peeled and finely chopped
- ¼ tsp dried chilli flakes, or to taste

To garnish:
- lemon rind strips
- red chilli slices

3

1 Using a sharp knife, trim the chicken, discarding any fat and cut into thin strips, about 5 cm/2 inch long and 1 cm/½ inch wide. Place in a shallow dish. Lightly whisk the egg white and 1 tablespoon of the cornflour together until smooth. Pour over the chicken strips and mix well until coated evenly. Leave to marinate in the refrigerator for at least 20 minutes.

2 When ready to cook, drain the chicken and reserve. Heat a wok or large frying pan, add the oil and when hot, add the chicken and stir-fry for 1–2 minutes, or until the chicken has turned white. Using a slotted spoon, remove from the wok and reserve.

3 Wipe the wok clean and return to the heat. Add the chicken stock, lemon juice, soy sauce, Chinese rice wine or sherry, sugar, garlic and chilli flakes and bring to the boil. Blend the remaining cornflour with 1 tablespoon of water and stir into the stock. Simmer for 1 minute.

4 Return the chicken to the wok and continue simmering for a further 2–3 minutes, or until the chicken is tender and the sauce has thickened. Garnish with lemon strips and red chilli slices. Serve immediately.

Sweet & Sour Fish

Ingredients
Serves 4

125 g/4 oz carrot, peeled and cut into julienne strips
125 g/4 oz red or green pepper
125 g/4 oz mangetout, cut in half diagonally
125 g/4 oz frozen peas, thawed
2–3 spring onions, trimmed and sliced diagonally into 5 cm/2 inch pieces
450 g/1 lb small thin skinless plaice fillets
1½–2 tbsp cornflour
vegetable oil for frying
sprigs of fresh coriander, to garnish

For the sweet & sour sauce:

2 tsp cornflour
300 ml/½ pint fish or chicken stock
4 cm/1½ inch piece fresh root ginger, peeled and finely sliced
2 tbsp soy sauce
2 tbsp rice wine vinegar or dry sherry
2 tbsp tomato ketchup or tomato concentrate
2 tbsp Chinese rice vinegar or cider vinegar
1½ tbsp soft light brown sugar

1 Make the sauce. Place the cornflour in a saucepan and gradually whisk in the stock. Stir in the remaining sauce ingredients and bring to the boil, stirring, until the sauce thickens. Simmer for 2 minutes, then remove from the heat and reserve.

2 Bring a saucepan of water to the boil. Add the carrot, return to the boil and cook for 3 minutes. Add the pepper and cook for 1 minute. Add the mangetout and peas and cook for 30 seconds. Drain, rinse under cold running water and drain again, then add to the sweet and sour sauce with the spring onions.

3 Using a sharp knife, make crisscross slashes across the top of each fish fillet then lightly coat on both sides with the cornflour.

4 Pour enough oil into a large wok to come 5 cm/2 inches up the side. Heat to 190°C/375°F, or until a cube of bread browns in 30 seconds. Fry the fish fillets, 2 at a time, for 3–5 minutes, or until crisp and golden, turning once. Using a fish slice, remove and drain on absorbent kitchen paper. Keep warm.

5 Bring the sweet and sour sauce to the boil, stirring constantly. Arrange the fish fillets on a warmed platter and pour over the hot sauce. Garnish with sprigs of coriander and serve immediately.

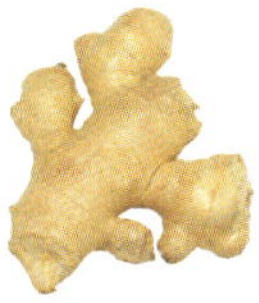

Sweet & Sour Rice with Chicken

Ingredients

Serves 4

- 4 spring onions
- 2 tsp sesame oil
- 1 tsp Chinese five spice powder
- 450 g/1 lb chicken breast, cut into cubes
- 1 tbsp oil
- 1 garlic clove, peeled and crushed
- 1 medium onion, peeled and sliced into thin wedges
- 225 g/8 oz long-grain white rice
- 600 ml/1 pint water
- 4 tbsp tomato ketchup
- 1 tbsp tomato purée
- 2 tbsp honey
- 1 tbsp vinegar
- 1 tbsp dark soy sauce
- 1 carrot, peeled and cut into matchsticks

1 Trim the spring onions, then cut lengthways into fine strips. Drop into a large bowl of iced water and reserve.

2 Mix together the sesame oil and Chinese five spice powder and use to rub into the cubed chicken. Heat the wok, then add the oil and when hot, cook the garlic and onion for 2–3 minutes, or until transparent and softened.

3 Add the chicken and stir-fry over a medium-high heat until the chicken is golden and cooked through. Using a slotted spoon, remove from the wok and keep warm.

4 Stir the rice into the wok and add the water, tomato ketchup, tomato purée, honey, vinegar and soy sauce. Stir well to mix. Bring to the boil, then simmer until almost all of the liquid is absorbed. Stir in the carrot and reserved chicken and continue to cook for 3–4 minutes.

5 Drain the spring onions, which will have become curly. Garnish with the spring onion curls and serve immediately with the rice and chicken.

CHEF'S TIP

Rinsing the rice in cold water before cooking will remove excess starch without removing the flavour, and will prevent the dish from becoming gloopy.

2

3

4

Sweet & Sour Spareribs

Ingredients

Serves 4

- 1.6 kg/3½ lb pork spareribs
- 4 tbsp clear honey
- 1 tbsp Worcestershire sauce
- 1 tsp Chinese five spice powder
- 4 tbsp soy sauce
- 2½ tbsp dry sherry
- 1 tsp chilli sauce
- 2 garlic cloves, peeled and chopped
- 1½ tbsp tomato purée
- 1 tsp dry mustard powder (optional)
- spring onion curls, to garnish

2

4

1 Preheat the oven to 200°C/400°F/Gas Mark 6, 15 minutes before cooking. If necessary, place the ribs on a chopping board and using a sharp knife, cut the joint in between the ribs, to form single ribs. Place the ribs in a shallow dish in a single layer.

2 Spoon the honey, the Worcestershire sauce, Chinese five spice powder with the soy sauce, sherry and chilli sauce into a small saucepan and heat gently, stirring until smooth. Stir in the chopped garlic, the tomato purée and mustard powder, if using.

3 Pour the honey mixture over ribs and spoon over until the ribs are coated evenly. Cover with clingfilm and leave to marinate overnight in the refrigerator, occasionally spooning the marinade over the ribs.

4 When ready to cook, remove the ribs from the marinade and place in a shallow roasting tin. Spoon over a little of the marinade and reserve the remainder. Place the spareribs in the preheated oven and cook for 35–40 minutes, or until cooked and the outsides are crisp. Baste occasionally with the reserved marinade during cooking. Garnish with a few spring onion curls and serve immediately, either as a starter or as a meat accompaniment.

Sweet & Sour Turkey

Ingredients

Serves 4

- 2 tbsp groundnut oil
- 2 garlic cloves, peeled and chopped
- 1 tbsp freshly grated root ginger
- 4 spring onions, trimmed and cut into 4 cm/1½ inch lengths
- 450 g/1 lb turkey breast, skinned and cut into strips
- 1 red pepper, deseeded and cut into 2.5 cm/1 inch squares
- 225 g/8 oz canned water chestnuts, drained
- 150 ml/¼ pint chicken stock
- 2 tbsp Chinese rice wine
- 3 tbsp light soy sauce
- 2 tsp dark soy sauce
- 2 tbsp tomato paste
- 2 tbsp white wine vinegar
- 1 tbsp sugar
- 1 tbsp cornflour
- egg-fried rice, to serve

CHEF'S TIP

Though this recipe is for turkey, the sweet and sour sauce works equally well with chicken, pork or fish fillets. If using fish, fry the fillets separately and pour the sauce over at the end.

1 Heat the wok over a high heat, add the oil and when hot, add the garlic, ginger and spring onions, stir-fry for 20 seconds.

2 Add the turkey to the wok and stir-fry for 2 minutes, or until beginning to colour. Add the peppers and water chestnuts and stir-fry for a further 2 minutes.

3 Mix the chicken stock, Chinese rice wine, light and dark soy sauce, tomato paste, white wine vinegar and the sugar together in a small jug or bowl. Add the mixture to the wok, stir and bring the sauce to the boil.

4 Mix together the cornflour with 2 tablespoons of water and add to the wok. Reduce the heat and simmer for 3 minutes, or until the turkey is cooked thoroughly and the sauce slightly thickened and glossy. Serve immediately with egg-fried rice.

2

3

4

Sweetcorn & Crab Soup

Ingredients
Serves 4

- 450 g/1 lb fresh corn-on-the-cob
- 1.3 litres/2¼ pints chicken stock
- 2–3 spring onions, trimmed and finely chopped
- 1 cm/½ inch piece fresh root ginger, peeled and finely chopped
- 1 tbsp dry sherry or Chinese rice wine
- 2–3 tsp soy sauce
- 1 tsp soft light brown sugar
- salt and freshly ground black pepper
- 2 tsp cornflour
- 225 g/8 oz white crabmeat, fresh or canned
- 1 medium egg white
- 1 tsp sesame oil
- 1–2 tbsp freshly chopped coriander

1 Wash the corns cobs and dry. Using a sharp knife and holding the corn cobs at an angle to the cutting board, cut down along the cobs to remove the kernels, then scrape the cobs to remove any excess milky residue. Put the kernels and the milky residue into a large wok.

2 Add the chicken stock to the wok and place over a high heat. Bring to the boil, stirring and pressing some of the kernels against the side of the wok to squeeze out the starch to help thicken the soup. Simmer for 15 minutes, stirring occasionally.

3 Add the spring onions, ginger, sherry or Chinese rice wine, soy sauce and brown sugar to the wok and season to taste with salt and pepper. Simmer for a further 5 minutes, stirring occasionally.

4 Blend the cornflour with 1 tablespoon of cold water to form a smooth paste and whisk into the soup. Return to the boil, then simmer over a medium heat until thickened.

5 Add the crabmeat, stirring until blended. Beat the egg white with the sesame oil and stir into the soup in a slow steady stream, stirring constantly. Stir in the chopped coriander and serve immediately.

Szechuan Chilli Prawns

Ingredients
Serves 4

450 g/1 lb raw tiger prawns
2 tbsp groundnut oil
1 onion, peeled and sliced
1 red pepper, deseeded and cut into strips
1 small red chilli, deseeded and thinly sliced
2 garlic cloves, peeled and finely chopped
2–3 spring onions, trimmed and diagonally sliced
freshly cooked rice or noodles, to serve
sprigs of fresh coriander or chilli flowers, to garnish

For the chilli sauce:

1 tbsp cornflour
4 tbsp cold fish stock or water
2 tbsp soy sauce
2 tbsp sweet or hot chilli sauce, or to taste
2 tsp soft light brown sugar

1 Peel the prawns, leaving the tails attached if you like. Using a sharp knife, remove the black vein along the back of the prawns. Rinse and pat dry with absorbent kitchen paper.

2 Heat a wok or large frying pan, add the oil and when hot, add the onion, pepper and chilli and stir-fry for 4–5 minutes, or until the vegetables are tender but retain a bite. Stir in the garlic and cook for 30 seconds. Using a slotted spoon, transfer to a plate and reserve.

3 Add the prawns to the wok and stir-fry for 1–2 minutes, or until they turn pink and opaque.

4 Blend all the chilli sauce ingredients together in a bowl or jug, then stir into the prawns. Add the reserved vegetables and bring to the boil, stirring constantly. Cook for 1–2 minutes, or until the sauce is thickened and the prawns and vegetables are well coated.

5 Stir in the spring onions, tip on to a warmed platter and garnish with chilli flowers or coriander sprigs. Serve immediately with freshly cooked rice or noodles.

Teriyaki Salmon

Ingredients
Serves 4

450 g/1 lb salmon fillet, skinned
6 tbsp Japanese teriyaki sauce
1 tbsp rice wine vinegar
1 tbsp tomato paste
dash of Tabasco sauce
grated zest of ½ lemon
salt and freshly ground black pepper
4 tbsp groundnut oil
1 carrot, peeled and cut into matchsticks
125 g/4 oz mangetout
125 g/4 oz oyster mushrooms, wiped

1 Using a sharp knife, cut the salmon into thick slices and place in a shallow dish. Mix together the teriyaki sauce, rice wine vinegar, tomato paste, Tabasco sauce, lemon zest and seasoning. Spoon the marinade over the salmon, then cover loosely and leave to marinate in the refrigerator for 30 minutes, turning the salmon or spooning the marinade occasionally over the salmon.

2 Heat a large wok, then add 2 tablespoons of the oil until almost smoking. Stir-fry the carrot for 2 minutes, then add the mangetout peas and stir-fry for a further 2 minutes. Add the oyster mushrooms and stir-fry for 4 minutes, until softened. Using a slotted spoon, transfer the vegetables to four warmed serving plates and keep warm.

3 Remove the salmon from the marinade, reserving both the salmon and marinade. Add the remaining oil to the wok, heat until almost smoking, then cook the salmon for 4–5 minutes, turning once during cooking, or until the fish is just flaking. Add the marinade and heat through for 1 minute. Serve immediately, with the salmon arranged on top of the vegetables and the marinade drizzled over.

CHEF'S TIP
To make your own teriyaki sauce, mix two tablespoons each of sake, mirin, Japanese soy sauce, and sugar. Beat together until the sugar has dissolved.

1

2

3

Wonton Noodle Soup

Ingredients
Serves 4

4 shiitake mushrooms, wiped
125 g/4 oz raw prawns, peeled and finely chopped
125 g/4 oz pork mince
4 water chestnuts, finely chopped
4 spring onions, trimmed and finely sliced
1 medium egg white
salt and freshly ground black pepper
1½ tsp cornflour
1 packet fresh wonton wrappers
1.1 litres/2 pints chicken stock
2 cm/¾ inch piece root ginger, peeled and sliced
75 g/3 oz thin egg noodles
125 g/4 oz pak choi, shredded

CHEF'S TIP
Buy fresh or frozen wonton wrappers from larger supermarkets and oriental stores.

1 Place the mushrooms in a bowl, cover with warm water and leave to soak for 1 hour. Drain, remove and discard the stalks and finely chop the mushrooms. Return to the bowl with the prawns, pork, water chestnuts, 2 of the spring onions and egg white. Season to taste with salt and pepper. Mix well.

2 Mix the cornflour with 1 tablespoon of cold water to make a paste. Place a wonton wrapper on a board and brush the edges with the paste. Drop a little less than 1 teaspoon of the pork mixture in the centre then fold in half to make a triangle, pressing the edges together. Bring the two outer corners together, fixing together with a little more paste. Continue until all the pork mixture is used up; you should have 16–20 wontons.

3 Pour the stock into a large wide saucepan, add the ginger slices and bring to the boil. Add the wontons and simmer for about 5 minutes. Add the noodles and cook for 1 minute. Stir in the pak choi and cook for a further 2 minutes, or until the noodles and pak choi are tender and the wontons have floated to the surface and are cooked through.

4 Ladle the soup into warmed bowls, discarding the ginger. Sprinkle with the remaining sliced spring onion and serve immediately.

1

2

3

Index